A Family in Mexico

A pronunciation guide for the Spanish and
Indian names and words used in this book
appears on page 28.

Map on pages 4-5 by J. Michael Roy.

LIBRARY OF CONGRESS CATALOGING-IN-PUBLICATION DATA

Moran, Tom.
  A family in Mexico.

  Summary: Describes the life of a Mexican family,
resident of a suburb of Oaxaca, following especially
the activities of nine-year-old Paula Maria.
  1. Mexico—Social life and customs—Juvenile
literature. 2. Family—Mexico—Juvenile literature.
[1. Family life—Mexico. 2. Mexico—Social life and
customs] I. Title.
F1210.M693 1987   972'.74   87-3482
ISBN 0-8225-1677-2 (lib. bdg.)

Manufactured in the United States of America

  2 3 4 5 6 7 8 9 10 97 96 95 94 93 92 91 90 89

A Family in Mexico

Tom Moran

Lerner Publications Company • Minneapolis

Paula María Fosado is nine years old. She lives in the township of San Felipe del Agua, in the state of Oaxaca, Mexico. Her family's house has a yard with a lush garden.

Mexico is a large North American country. Its population is growing very rapidly. On the north it shares a 1,300 mile (2,100 kilometer) border with the United States. Mexico lies between the Atlantic and Pacific Oceans. It touches Central America on the south, bordering Guatemala and Belize.

Oaxaca is a large state in southern Mexico. It includes valleys, high mountains, jungles, coastal lowlands, and beaches. Many of the state's residents are Indians, descendants of the ancient Zapotec and Mixtec peoples that have lived in the area for over 3,000 years. The word *Oaxaca* is based on a word used by the Aztec Indians to describe this area when they ruled it 500 years ago.

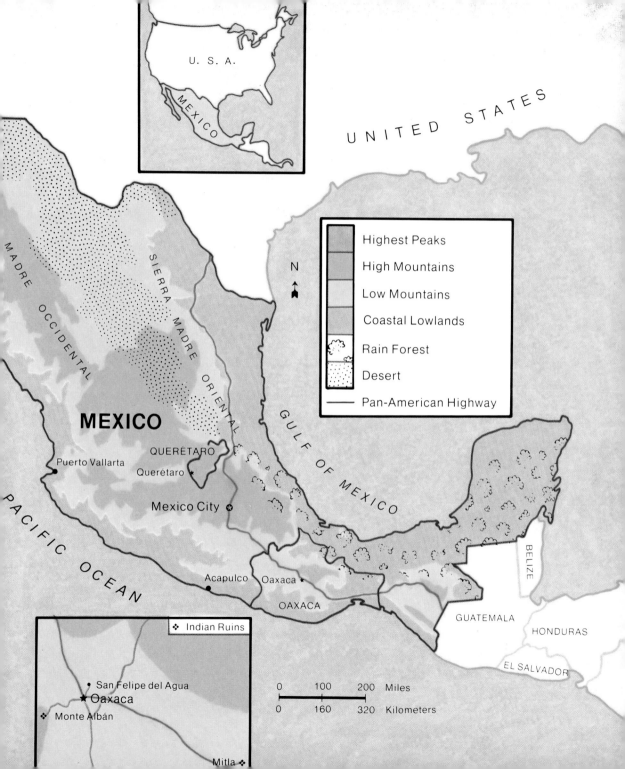

U. S. A.

MEXICO

UNITED STATES

N

Highest Peaks
High Mountains
Low Mountains
Coastal Lowlands
Rain Forest
Desert
Pan-American Highway

SIERRA MADRE OCCIDENTAL

SIERRA MADRE ORIENTAL

MEXICO

GULF OF MEXICO

Puerto Vallarta

QUERÉTARO
Querétaro ★

Mexico City ✦

PACIFIC OCEAN

Acapulco ● Oaxaca ★

OAXACA

BELIZE

GUATEMALA

HONDURAS

EL SALVADOR

❖ Indian Ruins

● San Felipe del Agua
★ Oaxaca
❖ Monte Albán

Mitla ❖

0   100   200   Miles

0   160   320   Kilometers

Paula María lives in a seven-room house with her mother and father. She has two older brothers and an older sister but they do not live at home. Her brother Ramón has just completed architecture studies in Mexico City. Her brother José Juan is studying at the school of graphic design in Querétaro, a state in central Mexico. Her sister, María del Carmen, is a student in the United States.

Parts of the Fosado home are more than 130 years old. They were built soon after Mexico won its freedom from Spanish rule. At that time the archbishop of Oaxaca made his home in the village of San Felipe. Some walls and outdoor water tanks at the Fosado home once belonged to the archbishop.

Most of the house is modern and was built seventeen years ago. It has red tile roofing, an open terrace, split levels, and two stairways to the garden. The old and new parts of the home blend together. Tiles inlaid into the outside walls state that the home is called "Quinta Juanita." It is dedicated to Paula María's grandmother.

San Felipe del Agua is a suburb of Oaxaca de Juárez, the capital city of the state. Informally, the city is simply called Oaxaca. It has 300,000 residents, and the population has doubled in recent years. Much of the city is very old and is built in a Mexican colonial style. For many years Oaxaca was the home of Benito Juárez, a famous Mexican hero.

The center of the city is the town square or plaza. In Oaxaca it is called the *Zócalo*. It is an open park area with fountains and benches. A large bandstand in the center is used for music concerts. The state governor's palace faces the Zócalo.

Nearly everyone in Oaxaca frequently visits the Zócalo. It is a very social place. When visitors come to the city from the nearby villages and outlying rural areas, they stop here to talk and meet old friends. Many of the visitors are Indians. The Indian women wear colorful clothing that indicates their tribe or village.

Paula María's father, Ramón, runs a business in Oaxaca that sells art and craft items. Oaxaca's natives are noted for their skill in crafts, especially pottery, woodcarving, and weaving. Much of this work is very colorful.

Señor Fosado's store is on a busy street very near the Zócalo. His assistant, Esteban, helps run the shop. The store is open until eight o'clock every night. Like most Oaxacan businesses, it is closed from 2:00 until 4:00 each afternoon for dinner. Paula María helps at the store. Sometimes she carries in the pots.

Many of the craft techniques have been handed down from generation to generation. Entire families, adults and children, become expert weavers or potters. Everyone in a village will help to carve, paint, or distribute the products of the local craft.

Señor Fosado often travels to the villages to purchase goods for his store or for special customers. He knows most of the artisans and their families. They like to show him what they are making and what they plan to have ready for his next visit.

11

When he travels to the villages, Señor Fosado often passes women and children gathering wood for their cooking fires. For many rural Mexicans, life is very difficult. Clothing is still washed on a river bank as it has been done for hundreds of years. Medical care is scarce. Often there is no electricity or running water and only a dirt floor in a family's home.

Farming is often done on very small plots of land. Sometimes the land was given to the *campesinos* or peasants by the government. Many farmers keep a tiny herd of animals like cows, goats, and sheep. Burros and oxen are often used to help plow the soil and harvest the crops. Hand tools like the hoe, machete, and sickle are used for much of the work.

In Oaxaca water is very scarce. The most common crops are beans, corn, and squash. Each year the small farmers hope there will be enough rain for their vegetables. If they are lucky, no disease or harmful insects will attack their plants. If the crops fail, life becomes even more difficult for the poor farmers and their families.

The Mexican government tries to help the poor people, but it is very expensive. Many Oaxacan villagers leave their homes and travel north to the United States to work. They are often separated from their families for a long time. Other farmers leave their villages to seek work in Mexico's big cities. Many discover that life is no easier there.

Each morning the Fosado family has a quick breakfast. Only on weekends is the family able to sit down and eat this meal, called *desayuno*, together. On weekends Paula María helps her mother prepare the food. She especially likes the rich hot chocolate. Chocolate is made from beans grown in Oaxaca state. Paula María stirs it with a special chocolate beater called a *molinillo*. It is made of wood and has sharp edges to smooth the chocolate drink.

Paula María and her mother, Carmen, walk to school each weekday morning. Paula María attends the fourth class of Escuela Primaria Beatriz Avila García. The primary school is named for a former teacher who taught there for 30 years. Classes start at 8:00 A.M. Paula María studies Spanish, social science, natural science, mathematics, and music. The school is public and all of the students wear a blue uniform. During recreation period Paula María eats a snack and talks with her teacher, profesora Yolanda León Ramírez. Afterwards she has exercises and games in her physical education class. Paula María loves the foot races.

School finishes at 1:00 P.M. In the afternoon Paula María studies and does her homework. Sometimes she studies at a friend's house. If the weather is good, she does her schoolwork on the terrace.

When she's through with her homework, she helps her mother with chores. Sometimes they walk down the dirt street to a neighbor's house. There they can buy *tortillas*. Tortillas are thin cornbread that are eaten at most Mexican meals. The neighbor makes them by hand from a flour mix called *masa*. She rolls the masa dough flat and then cooks the tortillas over a fire. She is called a *tortillera*.

When Paula María has finished her schoolwork and chores, she has some time to play. She likes to ride her bicycle around the streets of San Felipe del Agua. Sometimes she rides up the hill toward the old San Felipe parish church. The church was built for the area's Catholic *mestizos* in the eighteenth century. Mestizos are people of mixed Indian and Spanish blood. Each Sunday, the Fosado family goes to mass at the church.

Some afternoons Paula María's friends come to play in her yard or she goes to a friend's home. On weekends, she and her friends use the swings, slides, and rides in the playground. When her friends are busy, Paula María plays with her doll collection. Many of her dolls are handmade.

Mexico is a country of many celebrations and holidays called *fiestas*. Some are regional and are only celebrated in certain parts of Mexico. Oaxaca is noted for the *Lunes del Cerro* or *Guelaguetza* ("Monday on the hill," an Indian dance festival) and *La Noche de los Rábanos* (a radish festival and contest for local farmers).

Other fiestas are celebrated throughout the country. Some are religious, like the feast of the Virgin of Guadalupe, Holy Week, and Christmas. Others are patriotic, like the September 15 and 16 celebration of Independence Days.

Most fiestas are huge public celebrations. Usually there are processions and parades. School children, government employees, or the military might participate. Often there are fireworks, music, costumes, and dancing. The towns are decorated and men and women sell souvenirs, flags, and balloons. Visitors from the countryside travel to cities like Oaxaca to take part in the festivities.

Throughout Mexico, each town or village has a market day once a week. On that day, the farmers bring in their produce and artisans bring their pottery or handicrafts to sell. Hardware, clothing, and food are sold. Live animals like goats, pigs, chickens, and ducks are also sold at some of the markets.

Paula María and her mother like to go to the Oaxaca city market every Saturday morning. It is very large and crowded. People come from all over the city and from many nearby villages. Buses filled with people constantly arrive and leave.

Señora Fosado does the week's shopping. She carefully checks the fruits and vegetables, making sure she is getting the best quality. There are fresh bananas, tomatoes, mangoes, guavas, onions, melons, garlic, and jamaica, a red flower leaf used to make punch. Paula María and her mother fill two baskets with fresh fruit and vegetables before stopping at the meat counter to look at the poultry.

When the shopping is finished, Paula María stops at a stand to get a *memela*. It is a corn tortilla wrapped around beans, red or green chili sauce, and cheese. This is Paula María's favorite part of shopping.

On a mountain on the edge of the city of Oaxaca are the ruins of Monte Albán. These pyramids are all that is left of a Zapotec Indian civilization that flourished here more than 2,000 years ago. Paula María and her family like to visit the ruins. It is a reminder that the area and its traditions are very ancient.

Paula María's father maintains some of this tradition. On the outskirts of the city, farmers work the land with burros and oxen, depending entirely on the rains for water. In the garden that surrounds their house, Señor Fosado also raises everything without irrigation. The Fosados raise corn, tomatoes, carrots, radishes, onions, cilantro or coriander, and other herbs. There are also trees bearing figs, oranges, tangerines, grapefruit, pomegranates, coffee, and avocadoes. The yard is very lush. Paula María likes to help her father in the garden, working with the plants and trimming trees.

The Fosado family likes to attend Mexican rodeos. These are held on Sundays and are called *charreadas*. Señor Fosado and his sons used to ride in the charreadas. When Paula María is older she would like to ride in the women's events, called *escaramuza charra*. However, the Fosados no longer own a horse.

The entire family got together to celebrate the graduation of the son, Ramón, from architectural school. Paula María's grandfather arrived from Mexico City. Her other brother, José Juan, visited from college in Querétaro. They all attended a charreada at the Lienzo Charro, a rodeo stadium north of the city.

Charreadas include riding events, roping contests, bull riding, and Mexican folk dancing. They are exhibitions of superb horsemanship. The riders include men and boys, called *charros*, and women and girls, called *charras*. Some of the contests are very dangerous. In one contest for men, a rider must ride at a full gallop, grab a bull by the tail, and flip the heavy animal to the ground. This event is called *colas*, which means tails. All of the riders have great skill and respect for the animals. The women riders wear colorful skirts and blouses and ride sidesaddle. Many of the riders also participate in traditional dances.

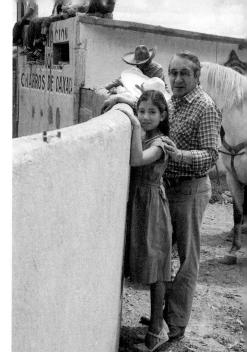

The Fosados held a large fiesta of their own to honor young Ramón's graduation. Many friends and relatives came to the house. There were many special foods, including *barbacoa*, goat meat cooked in an underground pit, and *cochinita pibil*, a Mayan-style pork dish.

The children played games in the lush yard and garden. One of their favorites is called *el juego de manos*, the hand game. The adults talked and sipped the special Mexican coffee, *café de ollita*, that Ramón poured. It is a very sweet ceremonial drink made with unrefined sugar and cinnamon. Paula María's father told everyone how happy he was for his son, Ramón. He said he was very proud of his graduation and glad that they could all celebrate this together.

After the sun went down, Ramón Fosado brought out a special handmade balloon. It was made of colored tissue paper. This kind of balloon is called *el globo*. It is an old Mexican tradition, popular with the campesinos, to launch these balloons to mark special occasions. A pan of kerosene is hung below the paper balloon. The kerosene is lit, and the hot air rising from the fire causes the balloon to rise into the air.

The balloon took off as the Fosado family and friends applauded. The bright light rose into the dark sky. Soon Señora Fosado told Paula María it was time for bed.

Spanish and Indian Words in This Book

barbacoa bar-bah-KOH-ah
Benito Juárez bay-NEE-toh HWAH-ress
café de ollita kah-FAY day oh-YEE-tah
campesino cam-pay-SEE-noh
charra CHA-rah
charreada cha-ray-AH-dah
charro CHA-roh
cochinita pibil co-chee-NEE-tah pee-BEEL
colas KOH-lahs
desayuno days-ah-YOO-noh
el globo ell GLOW-boh
el juego de manos ell hoo-AY-go day MAH-nohs
escaramuza charra es-kah-rah-MOO-tza CHA-rah
Escuela Primaria Beatriz Avila Garcia es-KWAY-lah pre-MAH-ree-ah bay-ah-TREES AH-vee-lah gahr-SEE-ah
Esteban es-TAY-bahn
fiesta fee-ESS-tah
Guelaguetza gay-la-GETZ-ah
José Juan hoh-SEH hwan
Juanita hwah-NEE-tah
Lunes del Cerro LOO-nes dell SEHR-roh

Maria del Carmen mah-REE-ah dell CAR-men
masa MAH-sah
memela may-MAY-lah
mestizo mess-TEE-soh
Mixtec MEEX-teck
molinillo moh-lee-NEE-yoh
Monte Albán MON-teh ahl-BAHN
Noche de los Rábanos NO-chay day lohs RAH-bah-nohs
Oaxaca wah-HAH-kah
Paula María Fosado POW-lah mah-REE-ah foh-SAH-doh
Profesora Yolanda León Ramírez pro-feh-SOR-ah yoh-LAHN-dah LAY-ohn rah-MEER-ess
Querétaro keh-REH-tah-roh
quinta KEEN-tah
Ramón rah-MOHN
San Felipe del Agua sahn fay-LEE-pay dell AH-gwa
señor seyn-NYOR
señora seyn-NYOR-ah
tortilla tor-TEE-yah
tortillera tor-tee-YEH-rah
Zapotec sah-POH-teck
Zócalo SO-kah-loh

Facts about Mexico

Official Name: United Mexican States (Estados Unidos Mexicanos)

Capital: Mexico City

Language: Spanish is the official language. Indian dialects are spoken in certain areas.

Form of Money: peso

Area: 761,604 square miles (1,972,547 square kilometers)

Mexico is about three times as large as the state of Texas, or one-fifth the size of the continental United States.

Population: About 85 million

The United States has approximately three times the population of Mexico.

NORTH
AMERICA

Mexico

SOUTH
AMERICA

EUROPE

A S I A

AFRICA

AUSTRALIA

31

Families the World Over

Some children in foreign countries live like you do. Others live very differently. In these books, you can meet children from all over the world. You'll learn about their games and schools, their families and friends, and what it's like to grow up in a faraway land.

An Aboriginal Family
An Arab Family
A Family in Australia
A Family in Bolivia
A Family in Brazil
A Family in Chile
A Family in China
A Family in Egypt
A Family in England
An Eskimo Family
A Family in France

A Family in Hong Kong
A Family in Hungary
A Family in India
A Family in Ireland
A Kibbutz in Israel
A Family in Italy
A Family in Jamaica
A Family in Japan
A Family in Kenya
A Family in Liberia
A Family in Mexico
A Family in Morocco

A Family in Nigeria
A Family in Norway
A Family in Pakistan
A Family in Peru
A Family in Singapore
A Family in South Korea
A Family in Sri Lanka
A Family in Sudan
A Family in Thailand
A Family in West Germany
A Zulu Family

Lerner Publications Company, 241 First Avenue North, Minneapolis, Minnesota 55401